walk with me.

a mother's story

a guided journal of memories
for my child

Other Books In The "Walk With Me" Series:

A Great-Grandmother's Story
A Great-Grandfather's Story
A Grandmother's Story
A Grandfather's Story
A Father's Story
A Stepmother's Story
A Stepfather's Story
A Sister's Story

wandering tortoise

ISBN: 978-1798604335

Introduction

This guided journal is a fantastic way to create a
one-of-a-kind keepsake for your child!

Includes over 125 thought-provoking writing prompts
written from the perspective of your child. Write as though
you are speaking directly to them.

Also Includes:

Four Generation Family Tree
Record the names and important dates of four generations!

Two Recipe Pages
Share those special recipes your family always asks for!

Two Dot Grid Pages
For drawing diagrams, floor plans, property boundaries,
room layout, etc.

Custom Prompt Pages
Each section includes a page to add
your own prompt or question.

Customize the pages with photographs, clippings,
and anything else you wish to include
to help bring your stories to life.

Family

Childhood

Teenage Years

Adulthood

Love & Marriage

Parenting

More About You

Looking Back

Looking Ahead

Your Full Name

Your Date of Birth

Your Place of Birth

the date you began this journal

the person you are completing this journal for

Family

Our

Your Paternal Grandfather

_____

B: _____ D: _____

M: _____

Your Paternal Grandmother

_____

B: _____ D: _____

Your Maternal Grandfather

_____

B: _____ D: _____

M: _____

Your Maternal Grandmother

_____

B: _____ D: _____

Your Father

_____

B: _____ D: _____

M: _____

Your Mother

_____

B: _____ D: _____

B = Born
M = Married
D = Died

Family Tree

You

_____

B: _____

My Father

_____

B: _____ D: _____

M:

Your Children

(me) _____

B: _____

_____

B: _____ D: _____

_____

B: _____ D: _____

_____

B: _____ D: _____

_____

B: _____ D: _____

Where did your name come from?
Does it have special meaning?
Were you named after a family member?

_____

_____

_____

_____

_____

_____

_____

_____

_____

_____

_____

_____

_____

_____

_____

_____

Did you have a nickname?
Where did it come from?
What do family members call you now?

_____

_____

_____

_____

_____

_____

_____

_____

_____

_____

_____

_____

_____

_____

Describe your mother.
When you think of her, which of her characteristics stand out the most?

What is your favorite memory of your mother?

_____

_____

_____

_____

_____

_____

_____

_____

_____

_____

_____

_____

_____

_____

_____

Describe your father. Which of his characteristics stand out the most in your mind?

What is your favorite memory of your father?

Do you feel you more closely resemble your mother or your father? In what way?

Were you able to see your grandparents
often when you were young?
Where did they live? What were they like?

_____

_____

_____

_____

_____

_____

_____

_____

_____

_____

_____

_____

_____

_____

_____

Did your grandparents ever tell stories about their past?
What did you learn about them?

Did you know your great-grandparents?
Where did they live? Describe them.

_____

_____

_____

_____

_____

_____

_____

_____

_____

_____

_____

_____

_____

_____

_____

_____

Do you have any siblings?
If so, did you usually get along with them?
What is your relationship like now?

Were you the oldest child, the middle child, the youngest child or the only child? How do you feel this has influenced your life?

_____

_____

_____

_____

_____

_____

_____

_____

_____

_____

_____

_____

_____

_____

_____

How did your family spend quality time together?

_____

_____

_____

_____

_____

_____

_____

_____

_____

_____

_____

_____

_____

_____

_____

_____

What do you feel was the most important lesson your parents taught you?

*Knowing what you know now,
is there anything you wish your parents
had taught you but didn't?*

What expectations or aspirations did your family have for your future?

- Family -

Is there anything you wish you had asked your parents or grandparents? What is it and why? Is there anything you wish they had asked you?

Add Your Own Question

Childhood

What is your earliest memory?

Describe your childhood home. If you had more than one, describe your favorite. Was it small or large? In a rural area or urban?

_____

_____

_____

_____

_____

_____

_____

_____

_____

_____

_____

_____

_____

_____

Draw a layout of your childhood home or yard.

Did you grow up in a two-parent household, a single-parent home or with someone else? How do you feel this has impacted your life?

_____

_____

_____

_____

_____

_____

_____

_____

_____

_____

_____

_____

_____

_____

What occupations did your parents or guardians have? Did you see them often or were they frequently away?

Describe what a typical day was like in your home.

As a child, what did you want to be when you grew up? Was there anything that influenced this decision?

What types of chores were you expected to do? Was there a chore that you especially liked or disliked?

Did you get an allowance?
How much was it?
What did you typically spend it on?

Do you have a favorite holiday tradition
from your childhood?
What is it, and why is it your favorite?

_____

_____

_____

_____

_____

_____

_____

_____

_____

_____

_____

_____

_____

_____

_____

What was your favorite childhood toy, game, or activity?

Did you have any childhood illnesses or diseases or any notable medical emergencies?

_____

_____

_____

_____

_____

_____

_____

_____

_____

_____

_____

_____

_____

_____

_____

_____

Is there a frightening memory from your childhood that you still remember vividly today?

Did you have a favorite bedtime story when you were a child?

Did you have an idol or hero as a child? Why was this particular person your favorite?

What was your favorite meal growing up?
Who made it?
Do you still enjoy it today?

_____

_____

_____

_____

_____

_____

_____

_____

_____

_____

_____

_____

_____

_____

_____

If you know the recipe, please share it.

Recipe: _____

# of Servings: _____

Ingredients:

_____   _____

_____   _____

_____   _____

_____   _____

_____   _____

Instructions:

_____

_____

_____

_____

_____

_____

_____

_____

_____

Who or what do you remember most fondly from your childhood?

_____

_____

_____

_____

_____

_____

_____

_____

_____

_____

_____

_____

_____

Add Your Own Question

Teenage Years

What school did you attend during your teenage years? Did you enjoy school? Would you have preferred a different school?

What was your school dress code? Describe what you would typically wear to school.

Did you participate in school sports, clubs or other school activities?

Describe your typical school day.

What was your favorite school subject or your favorite teacher? Why?

What school subject did you find the easiest? What subject was the most challenging for you?

Did you participate in a youth group or youth organization? How has this experience influenced your adult life?

_____

_____

_____

_____

_____

_____

_____

_____

_____

_____

_____

_____

_____

_____

_____

What trends or fads were popular when you were young? Did you participate in those fads?

_____

_____

_____

_____

_____

_____

_____

_____

_____

_____

_____

_____

_____

_____

_____

_____

Did you have a best friend
or group of friends as a teenager?
What things would you do together?

_____

_____

_____

_____

_____

_____

_____

_____

_____

_____

_____

_____

_____

_____

_____

_____

What did you and your friends like to do for fun? Did you have a favorite hangout?

_____

_____

_____

_____

_____

_____

_____

_____

_____

_____

_____

_____

_____

_____

_____

_____

_____

What types of music did you like back then? Who are some of your favorite musicians or bands from your teenage years?

How old were you when you started dating? Where did you typically go on dates?

Did you have a curfew? What time was it? What would happen if you missed curfew?

Did you have a job when you were a teenager?
What was it? How much were you paid?
What responsibilities did you have?

_____

_____

_____

_____

_____

_____

_____

_____

_____

_____

_____

_____

_____

_____

At any time during your youth, did you save your money for something special? What was it? How did you earn the money for it?

Did you ever get into trouble as a teenager? What kinds of consequences would you face?

When you were a teenager, did you have any idea what path you wanted to take after high school? What influenced your decision?

Add Your Own Question

Adulthood

How did you feel when you ventured out to live on your own for the first time?

Did you receive any education or training beyond high school? What was it? Did you earn any degrees or certifications?

_____

_____

_____

_____

_____

_____

_____

_____

_____

_____

_____

_____

_____

_____

_____

_____

What organizations or groups have you belonged to as an adult? How did you become involved in them?

What jobs have you had in your adult life?

What was your favorite job?
How much did the job pay?
Why was it your favorite?

_____

_____

_____

_____

_____

_____

_____

_____

_____

_____

_____

_____

_____

_____

_____

_____

_____

Can you drive a car?
Who taught you to drive?

When did you get your first car?
What make and model was it?
How did having a car change your lifestyle?

_____

_____

_____

_____

_____

_____

_____

_____

_____

_____

_____

_____

_____

_____

_____

_____

_____

Did you serve in the military? If so, in what branch of service? For how long? What was your rank? Where were you stationed?

What is a memorable moment from your time in the military?

Describe your first house or apartment. What did you do to make it a home?

Draw a layout of your first home or apartment.

When did you feel you were really an adult and not just playing the part?

Add Your Own Question

Love &
Marriage

In your own words, tell me what love is.
Has your definition of "love" changed
through the years? If so, how?

How many serious personal relationships have you been in?
What did you learn from them?

Tell me about the hardest breakup you've experienced. How did you heal from it?

_____

_____

_____

_____

_____

_____

_____

_____

_____

_____

_____

_____

_____

_____

When and how did you meet my father?
How old were the two of you?
What was it about him that attracted you?

What is your favorite memory about my father?

Was my father able to meet your parents? What was their impression of him?

_____

_____

_____

_____

_____

_____

_____

_____

_____

_____

_____

Did you get married?
What made you feel sure you chose
the right person to be your life partner?

Describe your wedding ceremony.
Who was there to celebrate with you?

Did you have a honeymoon?
If so, where did you go?
Tell me a fun memory of your honeymoon.

_____

_____

_____

_____

_____

_____

_____

_____

_____

_____

_____

_____

_____

_____

_____

_____

Were you married more than once? How do you feel those marriages differed from each other?

What is the most difficult relationship challenge you have had to face? Were you able to overcome it? How?

_____

_____

_____

_____

_____

_____

_____

_____

_____

_____

_____

_____

_____

_____

_____

_____

_____

_____

What advice about relationships, love and marriage can you share with me?

_____

_____

_____

_____

_____

_____

_____

_____

_____

_____

_____

_____

_____

_____

_____

_____

Add Your Own Question

Parenting

How did you feel when you realized
you were going to be a mother?
Who was the first person you told?

Tell me about the day
I came into your life.

How did you choose my name? Am I named after someone special? What would you have named me if I were a different gender?

_____

_____

_____

_____

_____

_____

_____

_____

_____

_____

_____

_____

_____

_____

_____

_____

Were you given any parenting advice?
What was the advice?
Who gave it to you?

What is something
I would do that tested your patience?
How did you cope?

Do you feel you have been a strict parent or a lenient parent? Why do you feel that way?

Is your parenting style similar to the way you were raised or is it different? Is that by choice or circumstance?

What do you feel is the most difficult part of raising a child?

What was your scariest moment as a mother?

Describe a rewarding moment in your life as a mother.

Some moms work outside of the home and some moms stay home or work from home. Did you like your arrangement? What would you change?

Is there a favorite family recipe you make?
Where did it come from?
How did it become your specialty?

Please share your special recipe.

Recipe: _____

# of Servings: _____

Ingredients:

_____   _____

_____   _____

_____   _____

_____   _____

_____   _____

Instructions:

_____

_____

_____

_____

_____

_____

_____

_____

At what point in our relationship do you feel we were the closest?

What point in our relationship do you feel was the most difficult for you?

What is your favorite thing about being a mother?

If you could turn back time, would you choose to raise your family differently? If so, what would you change?

Add Your Own Question

More About You

How would you describe yourself? How do you feel others would describe you? Why?

Is there anything about yourself that you would change if you could? What is it and why?

_____
_____
_____
_____
_____
_____
_____
_____
_____
_____
_____
_____
_____
_____
_____

What hobbies do you have?
How did you become interested in these hobbies?

_____

_____

_____

_____

_____

_____

_____

_____

_____

_____

_____

_____

_____

_____

_____

_____

Do you know how to play a musical instrument? How long have you played it? Is there an instrument you would like to learn to play?

Have you received any special awards
or recognitions in your life? What were they,
and when did you receive them?

Do you practice a religion? If so, is it the same religion as your parents and grandparents?

How do you feel religion has influenced your life?

What is your favorite holiday?
What do you love about it?

Who is your best friend?
How long have you known them?
What draws you to them?

_____

_____

_____

_____

_____

_____

_____

_____

_____

_____

_____

_____

_____

_____

What are your "good habits"?
Do you have any "bad habits"?

Do you have a special or unusual talent?

Describe an occasion
when you were proud of yourself.

- More About You -

Add Your Own Question

Favorites

Food: _____

Cuisine: _____

Dessert: _____

Drink: _____

Candy: _____

Game or Sport: _____

Athlete: _____

Book: _____

Author: _____

Television Show: _____

Movie: _____

Movie Genre: _____

Actor or Actress: _____

Composer: _____

Song: _____

Singer: _____

Music Genre: _____

Animal: _____

Vacation Destination: _____

Thing You Can't Live Without: _____

Pastime: _____

Modern Convenience: _____

Place to Shop: _____

Gadget or Tool: _____

Flower: _____

Person in History: _____

House Style: _____

Color: _____

Artist: _____

Article of Clothing: _____

Motivational Speaker: _____

Type of Weather: _____

Way to Relax : _____

Warm Weather Activity: _____

Cold Weather Activity: _____

Season: _____

Holiday: _____

Car: _____

Thing to Collect: _____

Quote or Verse: _____

Looking Back

What has been your favorite age or stage in life so far? Why?

Have you traveled much?
What places have you been?
What has been your favorite place to visit?

What is your favorite vacation memory, either from your childhood or from a trip taken more recently?

What is the best advice you have received?
Who gave you that advice?

_____

_____

_____

_____

_____

_____

_____

_____

_____

_____

_____

_____

_____

_____

_____

_____

Tell about a compliment you have received
that has had an impact on your life.
Who gave you that compliment?

Tell me about
any pets you have had.

What do you wish you had done more of in your life? What do you wish you had spent less time doing?

Describe a difficult choice
that you have had to make in your life.
How did you reach your decision?

_____

_____

_____

_____

_____

_____

_____

_____

_____

_____

_____

_____

_____

_____

_____

_____

What are some defining moments in your life?

- Looking Back -

Name someone you wish you could see again. What would you say or do when you saw them?

_____

_____

_____

_____

_____

_____

_____

_____

_____

_____

_____

_____

_____

_____

_____

Regarding world events and politics, how do you feel the views of your parents and grandparents have influenced your own perspective?

Is there anything in our relationship you wish had been different? Is there anything you would like to change?

What do you like the most about your generation?
What do you like the least?

What is your
most embarrasing moment?

_____

_____

_____

_____

_____

_____

_____

_____

_____

_____

_____

_____

_____

_____

_____

What is something you feel you would do differently if given the chance? What impact do you feel this change would have on your life?

What social issues of today did you see during your childhood?
Do you feel things have improved?

_____

_____

_____

_____

_____

_____

_____

_____

_____

_____

_____

_____

_____

_____

_____

_____

_____

What are the most significant differences you see between the world of your childhood and the world today?

- Looking Back -

What hardships have you experienced in your life? What challenges did you face? How did you overcome those challenges?

_____

_____

_____

_____

_____

_____

_____

_____

_____

_____

_____

_____

_____

_____

_____

_____

_____

_____

Do you have any disappointments or regrets? Tell me about them.

Do you have any unfulfilled dreams? Something you have always wanted to do but haven't?

_____

_____

_____

_____

_____

_____

_____

_____

_____

_____

_____

_____

_____

_____

_____

_____

Add Your Own Question

Looking Ahead

What are you looking forward to the most at this stage in your life?

Describe what your perfect day would be like.

- Looking Ahead -

What goals or dreams
are you working toward right now?

What skills or special knowledge do you have that you would like to pass down to the next generation?

What are some new skills you would like to learn?

What do you hope I learn from you and your life experiences?

What family traditions do you hope I carry on?

_____

_____

_____

_____

_____

_____

_____

_____

_____

_____

_____

_____

_____

_____

_____

_____

- Looking Ahead -

Do you have any advice to share with me?

_____

_____

_____

_____

_____

_____

_____

_____

_____

_____

_____

_____

_____

_____

_____

_____

_____

- Looking Ahead -

Add Your Own Question

Made in the USA
Middletown, DE
07 April 2024

52658802R00111